IMAGES OF WAR

THE PANZER III AT WAR 1939-1945

RARE PHOTOGRAPHS FROM WARTIME ARCHIVES

Paul Thomas

Pen & Sword
MILITARY

First published in Great Britain in 2013
and reprinted in 2020 by
PEN & SWORD MILITARY
An imprint of
Pen & Sword Books Ltd
47 Church Street
Barnsley
South Yorkshire
S70 2AS

ISBN 978-1-78159-040-9

Typeset by Concept, Huddersfield, West Yorkshire
Printed and bound in England by CPI Group (UK) Ltd, Croydon, CR0 4YY.

Pen & Sword Books Ltd incorporates the Imprints of Pen & Sword Aviation, Pen & Sword Family History, Pen & Sword Maritime, Pen & Sword Military, Pen & Sword Discovery, Wharncliffe Local History, Wharncliffe True Crime, Wharncliffe Transport, Pen & Sword Select, Pen & Sword Military Classics, Leo Cooper, The Praetorian Press, Remember When, Seaforth Publishing and Frontline Publishing.

For a complete list of Pen & Sword titles please contact
PEN & SWORD BOOKS LIMITED
47 Church Street, Barnsley, South Yorkshire, S70 2AS, England
E-mail: enquiries@pen-and-sword.co.uk
Website: www.pen-and-sword.co.uk

Contents

Introduction

This is the second instalment of a new unique series detailing the complete history of the Panzer tank at war. *The Panzer III at War 1939–1945* is a highly illustrated record revealing one of the foremost German fighting machines of the Second World War. With comprehensive captions and text, the book tells the story of the production of the Panzer III through to the key battles in Poland, France, North Africa, Italy, Russia and North-West Europe.

Throughout the book it shows how the Panzer III evolved and describes how the Germans carefully utilized all available reserves and resources into building numerous variants that went into production and saw action on the battlefield. It depicts how these formidable tanks were adapted and up-gunned to face the ever-increasing enemy threat.

Between 1936 and 1945, thousands of Panzer IIIs were built. For the majority of the war this tank was certainly a match for its opponent's tanks and quickly and effectively demonstrated its superiority on the battlefield. In fact, it played a crucial part in the desperate attempt to halt the Soviet drive, and was also used with deadly effect in the West performing defensive operations.

The Panzer III was an ultimate credit to the Panzer divisions it served. The crews that rode and fought in this vehicle from the blitzkrieg days of Poland and France to the defeat at Kursk and the German retreat across Russia were proud of its effectiveness and reliability on the battlefield.

Chapter One

Blitzkrieg
1939–41

For the invasion of Poland the *Panzerkampfwagen* III, commonly known as Pz.Kpfw III, made its debut for the first time on the battlefield. This medium tank developed in the 1930s was primarily designed to fight other armoured fighting vehicles and as an infantry support tank, which included supporting the Panzer IV.

The Pz.Kpfw III variants A through to C had 15mm of homogeneous steel armour on all sides with 10mm on top and 5mm on the bottom. During the invasion of Poland tank commanders knew that this new Panzer would certainly be well pro-tected against their lightly-armed opponents. It moved out onto the battlefield with the sole intention of fighting with other tanks. It was initially equipped with the 3.7cm KwK 36 L/46.5, which proved more than adequate streaming across Poland. The Panzer III Ausf. A through C were powered by a 250 PS (184 kW) 12-cylinder Maybach HL 108 TR engine, giving a top speed of 32 kph (20 mph) and a range of 150 km (93 miles).

For the invasion of Poland only 98 Pz.Kpfw IIIs were available, compared to 1,445 Pz.Kpfw Is, 1,223 Pz.Kpfw IIs and 211 Pz.Kpfw IVs. This meant that eight Panzer IIIs were incorporated in each light tank company, but some divisions had none as a result. Nonetheless, during the early hours of 1 September 1939, the German army finally crossed the Polish frontier and began Operation White, the code-name for the German invasion of Poland. For the attack the German army was broken up into two army groups: Army Group North, consisting of the Fourth and Third armies under the command of General Fedor von Bock; and the Southern Army Group, consisting of the Eighth, Tenth and Fourteenth armies commanded by General Gerd von Rundstedt. From north to south all five German army groups crashed over the frontier. Almost immediately they quickly began achieving their objectives.

The entire thrust of the German army was swift and devastatingly efficient. Blitzkrieg had arrived. From the beginning of the invasion the Luftwaffe had paralysed large sections of the Polish railway network, severely disrupting the desperately-needed mobilization, which was still far from completed. The Poles were faced with the finest fighting army that the world had ever seen. The quality of the German weapons – above all the Panzers – was of immense importance during the Polish campaign.

Within a month the Polish campaign came to a victorious conclusion and the Panzerwaffe were heralded as heroes for their part in the destruction of Poland. The Panzer III had played a significant part in the crushing of the Polish army. Along with its powerful force it had engaged in an innovative new form of mobile warfare. The Panzer III's 3.7cm gun had proved to be more than enough firepower to deal with the Polish army tanks, which were grouped in light tank battalions and light tank companies. While the majority of these Polish tank men were patriotic to their last breath, they were outclassed by the Panzer. However, they still managed to destroy a number of German vehicles as they simultaneously defended their country from both the might of the Germans and then the Soviet invasion from the east.

According to German figures, the Panzerwaffe lost some 1,000 fighting vehicles, most of which were knocked out during the campaign by anti-tank guns. Only twenty-six Pz.Kpfw IIIs were completely destroyed.

While the losses for the Germans were considered relatively light, the Polish campaign had certainly taught them a lesson in tactical mobile warfare. It had demonstrated the speed and power necessary for the Panzers to achieve their objectives quickly and decisively. At the same time it had provided the tank crews and their commanders with real experience of using armour in battle conditions. Poland for the Panzerwaffe was a complete success, and from the lessons in the east they were going to turn their less under-gunned vehicles into some of the most deadly fighting machines in the world.

Eight months later the Panzerwaffe were again called up for action, this time against the west. For this attack the German army was divided into three army groups: A, B and C. The main strike would be given to Army Group A, which would drive its armoured units through the Ardennes, swing round across the plains of northern France and then make straight for the Channel coast, thereby cutting the Allied force in half and breaking the main enemy concentration in Belgium between Army Group A advancing from the south and Army Group B in the north. The task of Army Group B was to occupy Holland with motorized forces and to prevent the linking-up of the Dutch army with Anglo-Belgian forces. It was to destroy the Belgian frontier defences by a rapid and powerful attack and throw the enemy back over the line between Antwerp and Namur. The fortress of Antwerp was to be surrounded from the north and east and the fortress of Liege from the north-east and north of the Meuse. Army Group C, which was the southernmost of the three army groups, was to engage the garrison of the Maginot Line, penetrating it if possible.

Between the three army groups the Germans deployed twenty-nine divisions under Army Group B in the north and forty-four divisions, including the bulk of the armour, under Army Group A in the centre. Army Group C with seventeen divisions covered the southern flank and threatened the French position on its eastern flank.

Also distributed between the three army groups was the armour, which would lead the drive through Belgium, Holland and then into France. In total a staggering 2,702 tanks took part: 640 Pz.Kpfw Is, 825 Pz.Kpfw IIs, 456 Pz.Kpfw IIIs, 366 Pz.Kpfw IVs, 151 Pz.Kpfw 35(t)s and 264 Pz.Kpfw 38(t)s. The reserves comprised some 160 vehicles to replace combat losses and 135 Pz.Kpfw Is and Pz.Kpfw IIs which had been converted into armoured command tanks, which resulted in them losing their armament. The vehicles that had been distributed among the ten Panzer divisions were not allocated according to formation of the battles in which they were supposed to take part. The 1. Panzer-Division, 2. Panzer-Division and 10. Panzer-Division each comprised 30 Pz.Kpfw Is, 100 Pz.Kpfw IIs, 90 Pz.Kpfw IIIs and 56 Pz.Kpfw IVs. The 6. Panzer-Division, 7. Panzer-Division and 8. Panzer-Division consisted of 10 Pz.Kpfw Is, 132 Pz.Kpfw 35(t)s or Pz.Kpfw 38(t)s and 36 Pz.Kpfw IVs. A further 19 Pz.Kpfw 35(t)s were added to the 6. Panzer-Division due to the complement of a battery of sIG (*schweres Infanterie Geschütz*) mechanized infantry guns. The 3. Panzer-Division, 4. Panzer-Division and 5. Panzer-Division each consisted of 140 Pz.Kpfw Is, 110 Pz.Kpfw IIs, 50 Pz.Kpfw IIIs and 24 Pz.Kpfw IVs.

In addition to the main armoured force that made up the powerful Panzer divisions, various other types of armoured units were used. There were, for instance, four independent *Sturmartillerie* batteries, each of six *Sturmgeschütz* (StuG) III assault guns. This vehicle was constructed from two separate elements. Its powerful, short but heavy 7.5cm gun was mounted on the Pz.Kpfw III chassis. The 7.5cm gun was a much heavier weapon than could normally be carried on a standard Panzer III, but the extra space for the gun was achieved by dispensing with the turret and bolting the gun on a fixed mount with a limited traverse. This vehicle provided ample mobile anti-tank support for the infantry divisions, and would soon earn much bigger respect on the battlefield than the Pz.Kpfw III tank.

By the time Germany unleashed its might against the Low Countries and France the Pz.Kpfw III had gone through some radical changes of its own. It was deemed after Poland that all early variants including the Ausf. A, B, C and then the later D model would be unsuited to large-scale production and many of these were handed over for training purposes. The first Pz.Kpfw III to go into full-scale production was the new Ausf. E, of which ninety-six were produced. This vehicle had much thicker front armour of 30mm, a Maybach HL 120TR engine and new suspension and gearbox. It was also fitted with the new more potent 5cm standard gun. This L/42 gun was fitted on the Ausf. E, F, G and H variants.

Throughout the Western campaign the Pz.Kpfw III fought with distinction and was seen in a number of close-quarter battles with both French and British tanks.

Generally the tank did extremely well on the battlefield and once more exhibited dominance against its enemies.

With the success of the Panzer in Poland and on the Western Front, from 1 June to September 1940 the total number of tanks in the Panzerwaffe inventory rose steadily from 4,150 to 4,833. Hitler was particularly insistent on hastening the outfitting of the Panzer divisions, and outlined the particular need that the Pz.Kpfw III and IV be raised to a special level for manufacture.

For Operation Sealion, the planned invasion of the British Isles, some 180 underwater tanks were requested to be built. On 1 August 1940 there were ninety Pz.Kpfw III with 5cm KwK and twenty-eight Pz.Kpfw IV ready for service. However, within weeks, plans for the invasion were abandoned and the Panzerwaffe's plans were shifted from attacking the West to a much bigger and bolder plan: attacking the Soviet Union.

During a ceremony Wehrmacht troops can be seen at an unidentified barracks with a stationary Pz.Kpfw III. This tank's armament comprised a 3.7cm KwK 36 L/46.5 gun and co-axial 7.92mm machine gun. The Ausf. As through to early Ausf. Fs were equipped with a 3.7cm gun, which proved adequate during the campaigns of 1939 and 1940. These early Pz.Kpfw IIIs that saw combat were attached to units of the 1st, 2nd and 3rd Panzer divisions during the Polish campaign or were troop-tested between 1937 and February 1940.

During a military procession a Pz.Kpfw III can be seen moving along a road flanked by crowds of civilians and military personnel. This vehicle was primarily intended to fight other tanks. Initially designers urged that the 5cm gun be specified on all variants. However, the infantry at the time were being equipped with the 3.7cm PaK 35/36, and it was thought that in the interest of standardization the Pz.Kpfw III should carry the same armament, much to the detriment of the crews after 1940.

Two troops plan their next move in Poland. Parked next to them in the undergrowth is a Pz.Kpfw III. On a peace footing Germany's armoured strength consisted of five armoured motorized divisions, four motorized divisions and four light divisions. An armoured division was made up of 345 heavy and medium tanks and a light division was half that amount. It was these armoured machines that were going to lead the first lightning strikes into Poland. Note the white cross painted above the tactical number on the turret for ground and aerial recognition.

During operations in Poland an unidentified German unit can be seen halted in a field. The tank is a Pz.Kpfw III Ausf. C. The distinctive white cross can clearly be seen to distinguish between friend and foe, especially regarding aerial attack.

A Pz.Kpfw III Ausf. E during operations in Poland in September 1939. Note the white cross painted on the front of the vehicle's superstructure. This photograph was probably taken much later in the campaign as there were a number of tanks in the German arsenal destroyed or knocked out as a result of the white crosses, which made them easy targets for the Polish anti-tank gunners. Much later in the campaign Panzer crews were compelled to either paint over these white crosses or obscure them with mud, as in this photograph.

A new Pz.Kpfw III Ausf. G armed with the 5cm KwK L/42 gun and reinforced with the commander's cupola. About fifty of these variants were equipped with the 3.7cm KwK L/65 gun before the Panzerwaffe decided to up-gun this tank to a more powerful 5cm weapon.

Stationary inside a French town is an armoured unit. Parked between a Pz.Kpfw IV and a Pz.Kpfw II is a Pz.Kpfw III. The armoured drive through France was swift. Using highly mobile operations involving the deployment of motorized infantry, air power and armour in co-ordinated attacks had allowed the German forces to gain rapid penetration followed by the encirclement of a bewildered and overwhelmed enemy.

Two Panzer crew members of a Pz.Kpfw III are making adjustments to the vehicle's wheels somewhere in France in May 1940. Prior to the invasion of the West Hitler had made clear his resolution that if he was going to win the war rapidly in the West the new Blitzkrieg tactic should be instigated quickly and effectively. While he had been aware that his forces had overwhelming superiority in modern equipment against a country like Poland, he knew that France and her allies had a slight advantage in terms of both numbers of troops and matériel. However, the Panzer played a prominent part in winning operations on the Western Front.

Halted in a field during operations in France either in May or June 1940, a Pz.Kpfw II can be seen with a stationary Pz.Kpfw III. An impressive total of 2,702 tanks were used for the German invasion of the Low Countries and France: 640 Pz.Kpfw Is, 825 Pz.Kpfw IIs, 456 Pz.Kpfw IIIs, 366 Pz.Kpfw IVs, 151 Pz.Kpfw 35(t)s and 264 Pz.Kpfw 38(t)s.

Panzer men wearing their distinctive black uniform take a rest beside a stream during the armoured division's rapid drive through France in May 1940. In a number of areas German tank commanders reported that the enemy was simply brushed aside, having been thrown into complete confusion. In most cases the defenders lacked any force capable of mounting a strong co-ordinated counter-attack. British artillery eager to stem the tide of the German onslaught poured a storm of fire into advancing German columns, but they soon found that the Germans were too strong to be brought to a halt for any appreciable length of time.

Here a Pz.Kpfw III Ausf. E belonging to the 6. Panzer Division moves forward across a field watched by foot soldiers. This vehicle can be identified as belonging to the 6. Panzer Division by the very small 'XX' marking of the division to port of the driver's visor.

An Sd.Kfz.251 halftrack leads a column of motorcycles during an armoured unit's drive through France in May 1940. These fixed-type bridges allowed a constant flow of traffic to cross quickly and effectively with unhindered movement and were quite capable of carrying much heavier loads such as both medium and heavy Panzers.

A column of Pz.Kpfw IIIs are seen stationary along a road somewhere in France in May or June 1940. In order to reduce the threat of aerial detection these vehicles can be seen hugging the side of the road and half-concealing themselves among the surrounding trees.

Supplying an armoured column was paramount to the success of its operation. Here a Pz.Kpfw III has halted next to a mobile fuel depot preparing to take on fuel. Behind the tank is a Pz.Kpfw I.

An interesting photograph showing a Pz.Kpfw III Ausf. G on a training exercise. Note the soldier lying on the ground. Panzer crews were trained not to fear a Panzer running over them while under attack and were conditioned to shelter beneath an abandoned Panzer until it was safe to emerge.

During the campaign on the Western Front in 1940 stationary vehicles can be seen in a French town. A Horch cross-country vehicle can be seen along with Pz.Kpfw Is and two Pz.Kpfw IIIs. A distinct feature of the Pz.Kpfw III was its three-man turret. This meant the commander was not in any way distracted by either the loader or gunner and could fully concentrate on his own tasks to ensure he was maintaining situational awareness at all times.

Two *Gebirgsjäger* (mountain troops) rest in front of a Pz.Kpfw III that has been hidden in undergrowth to avoid aerial detection. The primary task of the Pz.Kpfw III was to fight other tanks but although it was a well-built vehicle in terms of armour, armament and mobility, it was not outstanding. However, on the Western Front in 1940 it proved its worth and was highly successful.

Inside a decimated French town. A number of vehicles can be seen halted here, comprising Pz.Kpfw I, II, III (probably either an Ausf. E or F variant) and Pz.Kpfw IV. Note the letter 'K' painted in yellow or white on the front of the Pz.Kpfw I, indicating that this tank unit is almost certainly attached to *Panzergruppe* Kleist.

Panzer III Ausf. E can be seen in a French town during operations on the Western Front in May 1940. The Pz.Kpfw III excelled itself during this campaign and fought well against very modest enemy armour.

At a mobile workshop, here is a Pz.Kpfw III Ausf. C. This vehicle can be identified by the type of drive sprocket and the location of the front shock absorbers which are positioned just below and behind the forward return roller.

A group of soldiers pose for the camera on board a Pz.Kpfw III. One of the easiest forms of transportation for foot soldiers without incurring fatigue before reaching the battlefront was hitching lifts on board motor transport such as tanks. Not only did it save time in moving from one part of the line to another, but disembarking into battle was often achieved very effectively, yielding results for the men.

A common sight during the Blitzkrieg of 1940 was the hasty erection of pontoon bridges across the rivers in France. Here in the photograph in the wake of an armoured column is a motorcycle unit advancing over a pontoon. Because of the large numbers of rivers and streams encountered during the advance, all kinds of bridging and river crossings were essential if the Germans were to successfully achieve their objectives.

A column of Pz.Kpfw IIIs during operations on the Western Front in the summer of 1940. Stationary and watching this spectacle of armoured might is a column of infantry on horseback. Note the turret hatches open on both sides of the leading Panzer. This was quite common during warmer weather periods to circulate air inside the often stuffy and hot turret compartment where three tank crewmen were seated.

An interesting scene showing a very long halted column of armoured vehicles. At least the first four tanks leading the column are Pz.Kpfw IIIs. A group of infantry with their commanding officer and tank men stare at the photographer. Air dominance in northern France was achieved very quickly by the Germans as this image suggests, as there appears to be no contingency for aerial attack on their column.

The first of two photographs showing soldiers on board a new Pz.Kpfw III Ausf. F. The camouflage of this vehicle is painted in overall grey, which was the standard colour of all Panzers until the end of 1941.

A soldier poses for a photograph on board a new Pz.Kpfw III Ausf. F. Note the tactical number '121' painted in white on a rectangular plate.

A photograph taken during operations in the Balkans in April or May 1940. A halted Pz.Kpfw III can be seen with a stationary motorcycle and sidecar combination. Note how muddy the roads are.

A leading Pz.Kpfw III can be seen with logs festooned along the sides of the vehicle in order to ensure the tank can cross difficult areas of terrain without becoming stuck, which would consequently hinder the advance. Much of the terrain in the Balkans was hilly and mountainous and often posed a problem for tank crews in maintaining the momentum of the advance.

Here a Pz.Kpfw III rolls across a wooden bridge during fighting in the Balkans in 1941. The vehicle appears to be heavily laden with supplies in order to sustain itself for the long drive.

A Pz.Kpfw III crosses a pontoon bridge destined for the front lines during the German invasion of the Balkans. As with operations on the Western Front, various pontoon bridges were erected across many rivers. Engineers would first position the pontoon boats (either inflatable or 50-foot pontoon boats) in place and then the bridging equipment would be erected across them in a surprisingly short time. Some of the pontoon boats were fitted with large outboard motors to hold the bridge sections in place against the often strong currents. However, because there were so many waterways that needed to be crossed by so many different divisions, the Germans found that they were running out of bridging equipment.

Most likely during operations in the Balkans in April or May 1941 a Pz.Bef.Wg III Ausf. E, which can be identified by the .30 MG mount, is seen crossing a pontoon bridge. As with many command vehicles, this tank is fitted with a dummy 3.7cm gun. Note the large frame antenna mounted on the engine deck.

During operations in the Balkans in 1941, an interesting photograph showing an early Pz.Bef.Wg III command vehicle. This Ausf. H variant is fitted with an early 3.7cm dummy gun. Note the pistol port which has replaced the ball machine-gun mount on the front plate.

Somewhere in the Balkans a Pz.Kpfw III can be seen advancing through a relatively deserted town. The Balkan campaign comprised the German and Italian invasion of Yugoslavia and Greece.

A knocked-out Pz.Kpfw III, taken during the last days of the Balkan campaign in the early summer of 1941. Three officers can be seen observing the damage to the tank which has obviously been knocked out of action by a British anti-tank shell. The crew has bailed out, fearing a fire or, worse, an internal explosion.

An interesting photograph showing a Pz.Bef.Wg III Ausf. H from Panzer Regiment 2 of the 2nd Panzer Division driving through Athens past the Tomb of the Unknown Soldier. Note the tactical number 'II N1' painted on the rear plate. This indicates that this is the vehicle of the commander of the signals detachment of the second battalion.

Chapter Two

Barbarossa 1941

For the invasion of Russia, code-named Barbarossa, the German army assembled some 3 million men, divided into a total of 105 infantry divisions and 32 Panzer divisions. There were 3,332 tanks, over 7,000 artillery pieces, 60,000 motor vehicles and 625,000 horses. This force was distributed among three German army groups: Army Group North, Army Group Centre and Army Group South. The main armoured punch comprised 410 Pz.Kpfw Is, 746 Pz.Kpfw IIs, 149 Pz.Kpfw 35(t)s, 623 Pz.Kpfw 38(t)s, 965 Pz.Kpfw IIIs and 439 Pz.Kpfw IVs.

Almost immediately the Panzer divisions exploited the terrain and concerted such a series of hammer blows against the Red Army that it was deemed only a matter of time before the campaign would be over. Yet, in spite of these successes, the Panzer divisions were thinly spread out.

For the first four months of the war in Russia the Pz.Kpfw III with its 5cm L/42 gun still proved its worth on the battlefield, but with the combination of the vast expanse of terrain and being too few dispersed along an ever-increasing front, constant break-downs became common. The weather too took a significant toll on its effectiveness, and as a direct result many tanks became frozen in the deep plains, unable to make any further headway. Another major setback for the Panzer III was that as the war in Russia progressed, its role changed drastically from a main battle tank to an infantry supporting tank due to the fact that its gun was not strong enough to destroy heavier enemy tanks.

By the end of 1941 the battle-weary divisions of the Panzerwaffe that had taken part in Operation Barbarossa were no longer fit to fight. Mobile operations had consequently ground to a halt. Fortunately for the exhausted Panzer crews and supporting units, no mobile operations had been planned during the winter of 1941, let alone for 1942. In the freezing arctic temperatures the majority of the Panzer divisions were pulled out of their stagnant defensive positions and transferred to France to rest, reorganize and retrain. Many Panzer crews had fought desperately to maintain cohesion and hold their meagre positions which often saw thousands perish.

By early 1942 the German forces were holding a battle line more than 1,400 miles in overall length, which had been severely weakened by the overwhelming strength of the Red Army. To make matters worse, during the last weeks of 1941 armoured units had not been refitted properly with replacements to compensate for the large losses sustained. Supplies of equipment and ammunition were so insufficient in some areas of the front that commanders were compelled to issue their men with rations. In spite of the adverse situation in which the Panzerwaffe was placed during the latter half of 1941, the armoured units were still strong and determined to fight with courage and skill. While they had expended considerable combat efforts lacking sufficient reconnaissance and the necessary support of tanks and heavy weapons to ensure any type of success, they were still strong enough to influence the situation decisively.

Over the next few months as the weather changed the war in Russia once again became more fluid and to the Germans' advantage. Many of the worn-out and depleted divisions were restored back to strength, while others too weak for combat were relegated to Army Group North or Army Group Centre where they were hastily deployed for a series of defensive actions instead. The best-equipped Panzer divisions were shifted south to Army Group South for operations through the Caucasus. It was entrusted to the two Panzer Armies — 1st and 4th — to spearhead the drive. By May 1942 most of the Panzer divisions involved were up to nearly 85 per cent of their original fighting strength and been equipped with Pz.Kpfw IIIs and Pz.Kpfw IVs.

A Pz.Kpfw III near Roslavl drives along a dusty road at speed during summer operations on the Eastern Front. Note the letter 'G' painted either in yellow or white on the front of the tank, indicating that it belongs to Guderian's *Panzergruppe*. The Russians tried desperately to hold on to the town of Roslavl, but under direct attack by seven fresh German infantry divisions, the defence soon crumbled away. Around the town a pocket soon began to form with Germans bringing up greater artillery concentration, while Red Army troops feebly tried to break out. Roslavl finally fell to the Germans on 3 August 1941. Guderian ordered a Panzer striking force of three divisions immediately away from the main battle to probe southwards and clear up stragglers from both Smolensk and Roslavl. The battles of Smolensk and Roslavl were one of the swiftest as well as one of the most complete German army victories in the East. Altogether some 300,000 Soviet soldiers had been captured in the Smolensk pocket. However, 200,000 had managed to break out and fight in Roslavl and surrounding areas further east.

A crewman poses for the camera on board his Pz.Kpfw III during the transportation of its unit by train from one part of the battle front to another during the initial stages of Barbarossa, the code word for the German invasion of Russia. Note the track links attached to the front of the vehicle for additional armoured protection. Panzer divisions were often withdrawn from the front and moved from one area to another. This was frequently the quickest and most effective way of moving the units, so much so that the enemy was not even aware that a division had been moved.

Two photographs showing typical pontoon bridges erected across a river somewhere on the Eastern Front in 1941. These heavy pontoon bridges were known by the Germans as Bruckengerat B. The pontoon boats have been lashed together and the bridging deck sections secured over them in order to allow traffic and soldiers on foot to cross. These bridges were more than capable of supporting various types of armoured vehicles, including the Pz.Kpfw III and IV. Construction of pontoon bridges remained a vital activity, especially to assist heavy armour, and a well-trained Pioneer Bridging Column could put one together in a matter of hours.

A Pz.Kpfw III during operations in the opening phase of the German invasion of Russia. Note logs have been attached along the rear of the tank. For the invasion of Russia, the German army assembled some 3 million men, divided into a total of 105 infantry divisions and 32 Panzer divisions. There were 3,332 tanks, over 7,000 artillery pieces, 60,000 motor vehicles and 625,000 horses.

A Pz.Kpfw III halted on a road somewhere in Russia during the summer of 1941. In the Soviet Union the sudden speed and depth of the German attack was an impressive display of all-arms co-ordination. The Soviets were quite unprepared for the might of the German onslaught. In some areas the mighty Panzers crushed all resistance and enemy units were simply brushed aside and totally destroyed.

A Pz.Kpfw III during operations on the Eastern Front in the summer of 1941. Although the Pz.Kpfw III was very successful in terms of armour, armament and mobility, the eventual distances which had to be covered limited its tactics as well as causing breakdowns and immense supply problems.

A Pz.kpfw III Ausf. E bound for the front lines waits for traffic to pass along a congested road. Note the support vehicles in column with the tank. Out in the field support vehicles made a vital contribution to the Panzerwaffe's drive, especially when leading units were far ahead of their column.

A long column of Pz.Kpfw IIIs on a road in Russia. Note the trailers they are towing consisting of logs. In central and especially in northern areas of Russia where the terrain comprised vast lakes, swamps and forested areas tanks and other vehicles found the advance hindered by soft marshy ground. As a result crews took to using logs to lie over the ground so that the tank tracks would not become bogged down.

A playful Panzer crew are photographed on board their Pz.Kpfw III Ausf. F. This vehicle belongs to the 2nd Panzer Division and has been rearmed with the 5cm KwK L/42 gun. Note the earlier cupola, which has been retained on this particular variant.

Two photographs showing the *Sturmgeschütz* or StuG III built on the chassis of a Pz.Kpfw III and used effectively in an infantry support role as a self-propelled gun. During the early phase of the invasion of the Soviet Union the StuG proved its worth, especially in clearing out enemy infantry from urbanized areas. However, it was limited by its fixed turret. During the early part of the war in the East the StuG vehicle always kept pace with the infantry and supported them in almost all roles of engagement.

An Ausf. B variant StuG III on the road with infantrymen on board hitching a lift. Often to maintain the speed of an advance the accompanying infantry were carried into battle on the tanks and other armoured vehicles. When they ran into stiff opposition, they immediately dismounted to avoid taking heavy casualties.

Fuel was the most important commodity required by Panzer crews to move their armoured units from one part of the front to another. Here in this photograph Panzer men are seen at a mobile fuel stop with 200-litre fuel drums preparing to fill their Pz.Kpfw III. Overhead a German aircraft can be seen approaching an airstrip.

A stationary Pz.Kpfw III on the road. Note the 20-litre jerry cans on board the vehicle, necessary to support the vast distances over which they had to advance on a daily basis.

A modified Pz.Kpfw III Ausf. F out in the field. The crew poses for their photograph before resuming operations. Note the Notek headlamp has been relocated to the left mudguard and the vehicle still retains its early model cupola.

Troops rest at the side of a road during the summer of 1941. A stationary infantry supply vehicle can be seen parked on the road. Behind them is an advancing Pz.Kpfw III towing what are probably logs in a two-wheeled trailer. Moving along another road near the tank is a further infantry supply truck with a full complement of troops on board being hastily transferred to the front.

A column of armoured vehicles comprising a leading Pz.Kpfw III and an Sd.Kfz.10 halftrack advances along a road. Note the unit markings on the halftrack painted in yellow indicating that it belongs to the 2nd Panzer Division. In October 1941 the 2nd Panzer Division was transferred to the Russian Front in Army Group Centre for its advance on Moscow. The division became an active component of the XL Panzer Corps of the 4th Panzer Army. During the Battle of Moscow, vanguard elements of the Division reached the outskirts of the city.

A column of Pz.Kpfw III Ausf. E or F from the 2nd Panzer Division on a congested road somewhere on the Eastern Front. Note the national flag attached to the engine deck of the tanks for aerial recognition purposes. By mid-1942 this idea was eventually phased out by crews as they found that the Red Army air force could easily target the vehicles.

A photograph showing the StuG III operating somewhere on the Eastern Front in 1941. As German forces advanced ever deeper into the Soviet Union they encountered stiffer resistance where StuGs and other armoured vehicles became increasingly embroiled in fighting for each village, town and city. During the first years on the Eastern Front the assault gun proved indispensible to infantrymen and the elite Waffen-SS alike.

Panzer IIIs advance through a newly-captured Russian town during Operation Barbarossa. For the invasion of Russia, the strongest army group, Army Group Centre, made a series of heavy penetrating drives through the Russian heartlands, bulldozing through the marshy ground to the main Russian defences. Within days of its first attacks across the frontier both the *Infanterie* and Panzer divisions had pulverized bewildered Russian formations, which led to a string of victories along the entire front.

A Pz.Kpfw III Ausf. J from Panzer Regiment 15 of the 11th Panzer Division moves towards a village in Russia. Note the letter 'K' painted on the stowage bin, indicating that this belongs to *Panzergruppe* Kleist.

A Pz.Kpfw III Ausf. G moves along a muddy road bound for the front. Positioned to its left is a battery of 10.5cm le.FH18 light field howitzers. The 10.5cm field howitzer provided the division with a relatively effective mobile base of fire. It was primarily the artillery regiments that were given the task of destroying enemy positions and fortified defences and conducting counter-battery fire prior to an armoured assault.

A knocked-out Pz.Kpfw III obviously waiting for a salvage unit to collect and take it to the rear either for repair or to cannibalize the parts for other tanks. This was common practice in the Panzer divisions, and became a matter of life and death for the armoured divisions fighting on the front by 1944.

A Pz.Kpfw III with members of the crew riding on board along a dusty road somewhere in Russia in 1941. The situation for the Russians looked grim. The ferocity of the German attack was immense and without respite. Stalin's insistence that his troops must fight from fixed positions without any tactical retreat had consequently caused many units to become encircled, leaving Panzer units to speed past unhindered and achieve even deeper penetrations.

A StuG III Ausf. B hurtles along a dusty road on the Eastern Front during the summer of 1941. For the invasion of Russia German factories were able to complete 548 StuG III vehicles. The StuG had a crew of four and came equipped with a 7.5cm StuK 37 L/24 gun capable of traversing from 12.5 degrees left to 12.5 degrees right. Even with the high losses of the *Sturmgeschütz* on the Eastern Front, the crews still had a high regard for their self-propelled assault gun as a decisive weapon of war.

Wehrmacht forces of the 11th Panzer Division advance through a village, but not before burning it down as it passed through. The division was then sent to the Eastern Front in Army Group South where it was part of XXXXVIII Corps (mot.) under the command of General Kempf. The division fought brilliantly in the battle of Kiev, and then in October 1941 took part in the march toward Moscow as part of XXXXVI Panzer Corps in Army Group Centre.

Inside a town in the region of Kiev a Pz.Kpfw III can be seen advancing along a road among crude roadside barriers erected by the civilian population. When the battle of Kiev finally ended on 21 September 1941 almost 665,000 Russian troops had been captured in the encirclement. Exhilarated by the fall of Kiev, the German 6th Army mercilessly pushed forward leaving a trail of devastation in its wake. Across the whole of the German front Panzer IIIs and IVs leading the drive hammered deeper and the guns of the infantry divisions lengthened their range. For the men of the Panzerwaffe Blitzkrieg had once again been imprinted on the battlefield and there was an aura of invincibility among the men at this time.

A very interesting photograph taken in the early phase of action on the Eastern Front showing an early Pz.Kpfw III Ausf. G which has been converted into the rare *Tauchpanzer* for the proposed invasion of England, code-named Operation Sealion. These vehicles had hinged watertight doors over the air intake on the side of the engine deck. The tactical number '1100' painted in yellow indicates that it is a command vehicle.

A common scene during the early days of Operation Barbarossa. Here a Pz.Kpfw III advances along a dusty road with foot soldiers and horses following in its wake. By July 1941 the Soviet army was so overwhelmed by the German onslaught, it now seemed that Hitler's grand strategy on the Eastern Front had yielded such astonishing results that the Soviet army would soon be conquered.

A Pz.Kpfw III advances along a road passing stationary vehicles and foot soldiers. During the summer weeks of 1941 the Soviets were quite unprepared for the might of the German attack. In some areas along the front units were simply brushed aside and totally destroyed. Red Army survivors recalled that they had been caught off guard, lulled into a false sense of security after escaping a number of isolated pockets. Now they were being attacked by highly mobile armour and blasted by heavy artillery. In many places the force of attack was so heavy that they were unable to organize any type of defence. In total confusion hundreds of troops, disheartened and frightened, retreated to avoid the slaughter, while other more fanatical units remained ruthlessly defending their positions to the death. This was the scene on almost every part of the Russian front between June and September 1941.

A Pz.Kpfw III Ausf. G from the 2nd Panzer Division has run into some serious trouble while attempting to cross a wooden bridge over a river.

Out in the field a column of Pz.Kpfw IIIs can be seen advancing across a field during the summer of 1941. During the summer period the Panzer divisions exploited the terrain and concerted such a series of hammer blows to the Red Army that it was only a matter of time before the campaign would be over. Yet, in spite of these successes the Panzer divisions were thinly spread out. Although the armoured spearheads were still achieving rapid victories on all fronts, supporting units were not keeping pace with them.

A group of Wehrmacht troops pose for the camera with a well-concealed Pz.Kpfw III somewhere on the Eastern Front in 1941. Between June and late September 1941 the Panzer and motorized divisions were more or less unhindered by lack of supply, difficult terrain or bad weather conditions and the campaign in Russia during this period seemed to be going extremely well.

A Pz.Kpfw III Ausf. J crossing a temporary bridge over a small river during operations in Russia. This photograph was more than likely taken in southern Russia, judging by the contrast of uniforms which look tropical.

A Panzer unit halted in a field prior to its movement to another part of the front. Following the surge of success by the Panzerwaffe, the armoured spearheads were losing momentum. Not only were their supply lines being overstretched, but enemy resistance began to stiffen in a number of places.

A rather blurry image of two stationary Pz.Kpfw IIIs. The crew can be seen with both vehicles. All are wearing their special black Panzer uniforms, which were very distinctive from the German soldier's field-grey service uniform. The uniform was first issued to crews in 1934 and was the same design and colouring for all ranks of the Panzer arm, except for some of the rank insignia and national emblems worn by officers and generals, and was specifically dyed in black purely to hide oil and other stains acquired from the environment of working with the armoured vehicles. Across Europe and into Russia these black uniforms would symbolize a band of elite troops that spearheaded their armoured vehicles and gained the greatest fame, or notoriety, of being part of the once-powerful Panzerwaffe.

A number of Pz.Kpfw IIIs, a Pz.Kpfw II and a column of Sd.Kfz.251 halftracks advancing into battle in September 1941. It was during this month that the Germans unleashed Operation Typhoon, the advance on Moscow. However, in front of Moscow the Russians had constructed formidable defences in preparation for the German assault on their capital. Thousands of tanks and artillery were emplaced in the ground up to their gun barrels. Many thousands of mines were laid in the path of the German armoured spearhead. Nearly a million anti-personnel mines and booby traps were set up to explode and kill or maim unsuspecting German infantry. In towns and cities along the road leading to Moscow the Russians erected thousands of crude defence barriers.

A common scene out on the battlefield showing armoured vehicles spread out across a field in order to minimize enemy aerial attack against their advancing column. While at this stage of the campaign the Germans dominated the skies, there were growing concerns by September 1941 that the Soviet air force was amassing a large amount of aircraft for its defence of the Motherland.

A Pz.Kpfw III has pulled up to a river during summer operations on the Eastern Front.

Here in this photograph a Pz.Kpfw III Ausf. E makes its way across a prefabricated bridge. In the foreground are two soldiers taking full advantage of the very hot weather during the summer of 1941.

An excellent photograph showing stationary Pz.Kpfw IIIs inside a deserted village in Russia in the late summer of 1941. The emblem painted on the side of the Horch cross-country vehicle indicates that the unit belongs to Panzer Regiment 18 of the 18th Panzer Division. The emblem comprised a shield with a white skull and lines of water in white. This division was disbanded in late 1943.

A Pz.Kpfw III moves forward along a road. Track links have been bolted to the front of the vehicle in order to help defend it against possible anti-tank shells.

A Pz.Kpfw III negotiates a stream during operations on the Eastern Front in the summer of 1941. In the distance along a road is a column of horse-drawn supplies being moved towards the front. While the Panzerwaffe boasted of having the most powerful armoured force in the world, the majority of the German force in Russia was still moved by animal draught.

Two photographs taken in sequence showing a column of Pz.Kpfw III Ausf. J. Note painted on the rear of the turret the markings of Panzer Regiment 18 of the 18th Panzer Division which saw extensive action in Russia during 1941 and 1942. During the opening phase of the attack the division crossed the River Bug underwater, with submersible tanks. This was the first time ever that tanks had been used in combat like this. The division fought as part of LXVII Panzer Corps, and over the next six months was involved in capturing Smolensk, Bryansk and the assault on Tula.

A Pz.Kpfw III negotiates a road along a mountain range, probably in southern Russia. For the invasion of Russia, Army Group South was commanded by General Gerd von Rundstedt who deployed his forces down the longest stretch of border with Russia. The front, reaching from central Poland to the Black Sea, was held by one *Panzergruppe*, three German and two Rumanian armies, plus a Hungarian motorized corps under German command.

A Pz.Kpfw III moving along a road probably in southern Russia during summer operations in 1941. Note the leading Panzer carrying 200-litre fuel drums secured on the engine deck. This tank mounts a short-barrelled 5cm KwK gun.

A Pz.Kpfw III rumbles along a road during Operation Typhoon in September 1941. The crew has applied foliage to the engine deck of the vehicle in order to try to break up its distinctive shape and protect it from aerial detection.

A column of Pz.Kpfw IIIs advances through a newly-captured town watched by some of the local inhabitants during the early autumn of 1941.

Armoured vehicles advance along a road through a village in the early autumn of 1941. Note the national flags draped over the engine decks of two of the vehicles for aerial recognition.

A Pz.Kpfw III advances along a road during the early autumn of 1941. Attached to the engine deck are the tank's provisions including logs for boggy terrain. The distances these tanks had to cover were immense and it was therefore paramount for the crews to carry as many supplies for the journey as possible.

Two photographs showing muddy conditions on the Eastern Front during operations in the autumn of 1941. By this time the weather had begun to change. Cold driving rain fell on the Army Group's front and within hours the Russian countryside had been turned into a quagmire with roads and fields becoming virtually impassable. Many of the roads leading to the front had become boggy swamps.

Another photograph illustrating the muddy conditions on the Eastern Front during operations in the autumn of 1941. Although tanks and other tracked vehicles managed to push through the mire at a slow pace, animal draught, trucks and other wheeled vehicles became hopelessly stuck in deep mud. To make matters worse, during November the German supply lines became increasingly overstretched, their vehicles were breaking down and casualty returns were mounting. Stiff resistance also began to hinder progress.

Two photographs showing Pz.Kpfw IIIs in the snow during operations in the winter of 1941 on the Eastern Front. Elsewhere both Panzer and infantry divisions were experiencing terrible conditions as the temperature along the front lines plummeted. Along the German front conditions had considerably deteriorated for the Germans. During the last two weeks of October weather conditions became much worse. Heavy rain, snow showers and enveloping mists made movement almost impossible, even for the Panzers. In front of these exhausted troops stood Soviet forces who were determined to defend their land to the last. Even when the Germans managed to break through their lines, the Russian rear guards never left their position until they were literally blown off it. Slowly the movement of the Panzers halted through fatigue, shortages and the freezing climate. In a number of places the Soviets then exploited the situation and attacked them without respite, pulverizing their positions with their *Katyusha* rocket-launchers.

During winter operations on the Eastern Front a Pz.Kpfw III can be seen halted in a village. This Panzer mounts a short-barrelled 5cm KwK gun with an external gun shield. Note that in spite of the extreme cold weather conditions the lid of the escape hatch is open, obviously to allow fresh air to pass through the often smelly and stuffy confines of the tank.

(*Opposite*) Three photographs taken during winter operations in Russia. By early December the situation for the Germans had become much worse as the temperature dropped. Many soldiers were now reluctant to emerge from their shelter during the blizzards to fight. Hundreds of tanks were abandoned in the drifting snow. By mid-December with the situation worse than ever the temperatures reached 40 degrees below zero. On the central front, for instance, where Army Group Centre had been fighting for Moscow, despair gripped the lines. On Christmas Eve General Heinz Guderian, 2nd Panzer Group reported it had less than forty Panzers in its entire command; General Hoppner had only fifteen tanks, and still they were told not to withdraw. Hitler's policy of holding his battered frostbitten forces in front of Moscow had in fact saved ground, but at an alarming cost in men and matériel. The Russians, as predicted, finally ran out of power because of the harsh weather and were unable to achieve any deep penetration into the German lines. This consequently saved Army Group Centre from complete destruction. Although Hitler was later to say that the battle for Moscow was his finest hour, his army had in fact failed to capture the city, being crucified by the Russian winter and by fanatical Soviet resistance. Much of the failure of Operation Typhoon was essentially due to the remarkable Russian recovery and their winter offensive.

The crew of a Pz.Kpfw III Ausf. J point skyward and wave their national flag for aerial recognition. Note the tank's whitewash which looks either quite worn or less than liberally applied. It was common practice, especially during 1941 and 1942, for Panzer crews to drape the national flag across their vehicle in order to prevent being attacked. This crew is certainly taking no chances.

Here a Pz.Kpfw III Ausf. J has halted in the snow during late winter operations either in 1941 or 1942. This photograph illustrates just to what lengths Panzer crews went in trying to blend their vehicle into the local surroundings. This crew has actually used what appears to be chalk and applied it to the tank's armoured body. While this type of application of camouflage never lasted long, it was nonetheless effective in snowy terrain.

A crewman can be seen handing a 5cm shell to his comrade through the side turret door of a Pz.Kpfw III. This is probably an Ausf. F variant, armed with the short-barrelled 5cm KwK38 L/42 gun. The Panzer has received quite a good coating of whitewash camouflage paint.

Two photographs showing the reality of the Russian winter of 1941. All across the front both troops and tanks had ground to a halt in the arctic conditions. The extreme winter of late 1941 had caused the German army serious delays. As a result, much of the front stagnated until the spring thaw of 1942, delaying the conquest of Russia by months.

Operation Barbarossa had been a success in terms of the vast distances over which the Wehrmacht had travelled, but coupled with growing enemy resistance and the Russian winter, it had failed to achieve its objective. Consequently, the winter battle on the Eastern Front had completely altered both the Wehrmacht and Panzerwaffe from their glory days in June and July 1941. From now on, both would carry the scars of that first winter to their grave.

Chapter Three

Russia
1942–43

The opening of the new *Blau* Offensive gave a great promise of success to both the German army and the Panzerwaffe in the summer of 1942, in spite of the massive losses inflicted on them during the latter part of 1941. As for the Pz.Kpfw III, this remained in production as a close support vehicle. The Pz.Kpfw IV, for instance, was increasingly becoming the Panzerwaffe's main medium tank because of its better upgrade potential. Even so, newer Panzer III variants were still coming off the production line in 1942, such as the Ausf. N which mounted a low-velocity 7.5cm KwK 37 L/24 cannon. This powerful gun was identical to those previously fitted to the early Panzer IV Ausf. A to Ausf. F variants. However, with the more powerful, more deadly enemy tanks such as the T-34 and KV, it was imperative that the Panzer III was re-armed with a longer, more powerful 5cm cannon. The earlier Panzer IIIs were generally no match against the T-34 until the Panzer was fitted with the new 5cm KwK 39 L/60 gun introduced on the Panzer III Ausf. J in the spring of 1942. This gun was based on the infantry's 5cm Pak 38 L/60. It was quite capable of penetrating the T-34 frontally at ranges under 500m (1,640ft). Against the KV tanks losses were high, but not to be deterred, some tank crews began arming their Panzer IIIs with special high-velocity tungsten rounds, scoring considerable successes in the field.

Nevertheless, in spite of the newer, more powerful Panzer III variants making their debut on the battlefield in Russia in 1942, nothing could mask the gargantuan task it would be to defeat the Soviet army. While the Panzer far outweighed the Soviet armour with its superior design and tactics, the Russians were already amassing huge quantities of tanks and supplies at the front; far more than the Germans could match with their own. Consequently, in some sectors of the front the Soviets had around ten times more armour attacking or defending against a meagrely scraped-together number of Panzers. Quite often Panzer crews undertook sterling offensive and defensive operations against the growing might of the Russians, and these yielded some surprising success.

Despite the stiffening resistance of the Red Army during 1942, the Panzerwaffe stood firm.

While the best efforts were made to expand the armoured force, during the second half of 1942 more and more Panzer divisions saw extensive action and were continuously being shuttled from one danger spot to another, with only a brief rest for refitting. The Panzer III, Panzer IV and the new Tiger tank, including the StuG III, were continuously committed to battle, where they supported troops and attacked. Sometimes the outcome was successful, but there were many times when they failed. Yet, whatever the outcome of the individual action, the end mostly resulted in blunting further enemy breakthroughs. This had become the value of the Panzerwaffe in late 1942.

While many of the Panzers were tied down along a battered and bruised front, more resources continued to pour into the Panzer divisions. Even when 1943 opened up, the Panzerwaffe still managed to build itself up a strength of the badly depleted Panzer force. By the summer they fielded some twenty-four Panzer divisions on the Eastern Front alone. This was a staggering transformation of a Panzer force that had lost immeasurable amounts of armour in less than two years of combat. Now the Panzerwaffe would be tested to the end of its endurance with what became the largest tank battle of the Second World War, Operation *Zitadelle* (Citadel).

A Pz.Kpfw III in the snow during winter operations in Russia during early 1942. By this period of the war the Panzerwaffe divisions that had taken part in Operation Barbarossa were no longer fit to fight and mobile operations had consequently ground to a halt. Fortunately for the exhausted crews and supporting units, no such operations had been planned during the winter of 1941, let alone for 1942.

A close-up view of the front underbelly of a Pz.Kpfw III clearly showing the dark grey camouflage scheme of the vehicle and its armament. For the first four months of Operation Barbarossa the vehicles painted in this way blended well with the local terrain.

A Pz.Kpfw III Ausf. H stationary in the snow. Standing next to the vehicle is a member of the *Feldgendarmerie* or Military Police. This variant belongs to the 7th Panzer Division as indicated by the divisional insignia 'Y' painted in yellow.

A Pz.Kpfw III Ausf. J from Panzer Regiment 31 of the 5th Panzer Division complete with winter whitewash moves through the snow bound for the front line. During the winter of 1941/42 any mobile operations on the Eastern Front gradually ground to a halt.

A typical scene on the Eastern Front. A halted Pz.Kpfw III can be seen on a snow-covered road. Standing in front of the tank is its crew conversing with Wehrmacht troops clad in white camouflage sheets over their uniforms. This was an early attempt by the Germans to adopt some kind of camouflage during winter fighting.

A knocked-out Pz.Kpfw III can be seen in the snow somewhere in Russia. By the end of 1941/early 1942 many tanks had either ground to a halt in the snow or were put out of action by mechanical breakdown or enemy anti-tank shells. The Germans had made no preparations whatsoever for the winter and the Panzer divisions lacked the most basic supplies for cold weather. There were no chains available for towing vehicles and no antifreeze for the engines' coolant systems. Tank and infantrymen alike had no winter clothing either.

A Pz.Kpfw III advances through the snow passing a village during the winter of early 1942. No attempt has been made by the crew to try to camouflage the vehicle in order to blend in with the white arctic surroundings, so it still retains its overall dark grey appearance. While winter whitewash paint was not commonly used during this early period of the war, a number of tank crews did use chalk as a quick and effective alternative.

A Pz.Kpfw III bound for the front during early winter operations in 1942. The Panzer crews that advanced through Russia were amazed by the immense forests, the huge expanses of marshland and the many rivers that were continuously prone to flooding. They were also surprised that the little information they did have was often incorrect. Maps frequently showed none of the roads and when they were fortunate enough to come across them, they were in such a terrible state of repair that military traffic would often reduce them to nothing more than dirt tracks.

A well-camouflaged StuG III has halted in the snow alongside a building in early 1942. By the winter period in Russia the constant demands of the war effort meant that the StuG was often being employed in single battalions or even single machines. This consequently led to high losses of the StuG in the first year of fighting in Russia.

A decorated crewman poses next to a Pz.Kpfw III during the early winter of 1942. He wears the special uniform which was introduced for both *Sturmartillerie* and *Panzerjäger* units. This uniform was designed primarily to be worn inside and away from their armoured vehicles, and for this reason designers had produced a garment that gave better camouflage qualities than the standard black Panzer uniform. The uniform worn by units of the *Panzerjäger* was made entirely from lightweight grey-green wool material. The cut was very similar to that of the black Panzer uniform. However, it did differ in respect of insignia and collar patches, the latter consisting of the death's head emblems which were stitched-on patches of dark blue-green cloth and were edged with bright red *Waffenfarbe* piping.

Two Pz.Kpfw IIIs which appear to be Ausf. Js or Ls. These vehicles were retrofitted with the L/60 version of the 5cm KwK 38 L/42. Both of these tanks can be seen moving forward passing destroyed Russian vehicles and weaponry which often littered the roads for many miles. Although the winter of 1941 took its toll on the Panzerwaffe, its recovery was swift and new plans were made for bold offensives in the East.

A knocked-out Pz.Kpfw III on the Eastern Front. The vehicle mounts the 5cm KwK barrel and the turret has been turned in order to defend its position during the fire-fight that obviously ensued. As with many armoured vehicles this one has used the building behind it to help conceal it against both ground and aerial enemy attack, but on this occasion without success.

An interesting photograph showing a Pz.Kpfw III Ausf. N which has run into some considerable difficulty in soft ground. This vehicle was one of 213 such variants to be manufactured on the new Ausf. M chassis. The tank has side skirts fitted for additional armoured protection against the growing threat of Soviet anti-tank shells.

Pictured here in a field is a Pz.Beob.Wg III. This tank was specifically used as an observation vehicle and was constructed on a chassis of a Pz.Kpfw III. The driver's visor identifies it as an Ausf. G variant. A dummy gun has also been installed and a periscope in the turret roof for observation.

A Pz.Kpfw III Ausf. H drives along a dirt track near Divisional Headquarters of the 5th Panzer Division in the spring of 1942. The tank is laden with provisions for its long drive and its hatches are open to allow the very warm air to escape from its often sweaty and smelly confines.

Two photographs showing Pz.Kpfw IIIs being transported to the front on specially-designed flatbed rail cars. The Panzerwaffe owed much of its success in Russia to the quick and effective movement of their armoured vehicles. In a number of cases whole divisions were secretly withdrawn from the front and hastily transported to another area without the enemy suspecting anything for days, only to find that the particular Panzer division had arrived somewhere else and was threatening their lines.

A Pz.Kpfw III on a road during the spring of 1942 in the area around Kharkov. By the time the spring thaw arrived in March 1942, the Soviet leadership was convinced that the Wehrmacht was overstretched. Soviet generals therefore envisaged a bold plan to further stem the German drive by unleashing a counter-thrust at the southern end of the front near the town of Kharkov.

A stationary Pz.Kpfw III with its crew taking a much-needed respite during the spring of 1942. Logs can be seen strapped to the rear of the engine deck in order to prevent the vehicle from sinking in the mire.

A column of Pz.Kpfw IIIs is seen in this photo halted on a road somewhere on the Eastern Front during the early spring of 1942. Wehrmacht foot soldiers are standing next to the leading tank, one of whom is wearing the standard army greatcoat and conferring with one of the tank men.

In this picture taken from another vehicle during the opening summer offensive, a Pz.Kpfw III is moving across a field bound for the battlefront in an ambitious offensive that involved the seizure of Stalingrad and the isthmus between the Don and the Volga. Following the capture of the city of Stalingrad the Germans planned to use the city as an anchor and send the mass of its Panzerwaffe south to occupy the Caucasus where it would be used to cut off vital Russian oil supplies. The directive that Hitler himself dictated was executed in two stages. The first part of the summer operation was a determined all-out drive in successive enveloping thrusts along the Kursk-Voronezh axis, where it was to destroy the Soviet southern flank and carry on to the River Don. The second part was the advance to Stalingrad and across the lower Don into the Caucasus.

Spread out in a field are a number of armoured vehicles including Pz.Kpfw IIs and IIIs. Even as the Panzerwaffe slowly recovered from the terrible winter of 1941, in the spring of 1942 Hitler was still examining his strategic options in spite of its first defeat in one of the coldest winters in recorded history. In front of his generals he boldly revealed he would yet again bear the fruits of success in the Soviet heartlands and resume an offensive that would leave the 'Russian bear' reeling in its own 'blood on the battlefield'.

Preparing for a drive eastwards in 1942 is a stationary Pz.Kpfw III. Behind it is a knocked-out Russian tank. In the spring of 1942 Hitler announced to his staff that his forces should be refitted with the utmost speed. Unlike the previous year, he said, when the Panzerwaffe had advanced along three strategic axes towards Moscow, Leningrad and Rostov, his forces in 1942 would concentrate on a drive through the Donets Basin into the bend of the River Don west of Stalingrad and then south into the oil-rich Caucasus. He confidently revealed that this concerted advance across flat, endless landmasses which were well-suited to armoured operations would ensure the complete encirclement of tens of thousands of Russian troops. The operation, code-named *Blau* (Blue), was supposed to be the key to the success of the German drive in southern Russia which was to eventually deprive the Red Army of the resources necessary to continue the war. Subsequently to achieve these ambitious ends Hitler sought to wrench open the southern front and clear a path for the Wehrmacht to begin its summer offensive.

Halted on a road in southern Russia is a Pz.Kpfw III, prior to this vehicle joining a unit for the planned drive on the city of Kharkov. Kharkov was one strategic city that needed to be held before the commencement of the *Blau* summer offensive. For weeks German planners meticulously strove to achieve the desired results and developed plans to eradicate Red Army formations that were surrounding the area of Kharkov before *Blau* could be unleashed. Although the Kharkov operation came as a surprise to most Germans who were about to participate in it, the timing of the attack, the strength of the forces that were moved into the battle line and the sophisticated strategic and operational planning brought an air of confidence into the German high command.

Watched by the local inhabitants of a small town a column of vehicles drives through, destined for the front. The leading tank is a Pz.Kpfw III armed with a 5cm KwK L/60 gun.

Pictured here is a Pz.Kpfw III Ausf. G which has got into serious trouble attempting to cross a bridge somewhere on the Eastern Front. The bridge has collapsed under the sheer weight of the vehicle. The tank had been fitted with a 5cm KwK L/43 gun.

Wehrmacht troops pose for the camera on board a Pz.Kpfw III Ausf. J during the spring thaw of 1942. Many troops, despite the terrors of the winter of 1941, were imbued with a new confidence that many had not seen since they had first unleashed their initial attacks against the Soviet Union in June 1941.

A Panzer crew with their well-concealed tank during operations on the Eastern Front. This vehicle has smoke-candle dischargers attached. The use of smoke-candle dischargers on Panzers was common until mid-1943. The use of smoke in the German arsenal was something the troops were taught during training and was often used as an initiation of surprise attacks.

A Pz.Bef.Wg III Ausf III which appears to have been converted into a *Tauchpanzer* as indicated by the curved exhaust pipes. This vehicle is moving towards the battlefront during operations in 1942 somewhere in Russia and is heavily laden with supplies for its long drive eastward.

A Pz.Bef.Wg III command vehicle. A special rack has been constructed on the engine deck of the tank in order to carry additional fuel for the long drive through the Soviet Union.

A stationary Pz.Kpfw III still retaining its original grey camouflage scheme. Its three-digit tactical number '513' can be seen painted in white next to the national cross.

En route towards the front lines in May 1942 is a column of armoured vehicles. Leading the drive along this dusty road is a Pz.Kpfw III. It was during this month that the Germans unleashed their summer offensive, with the first objective being Kharkov. By 24 May Red Army formations had found themselves completely encircled near Kharkov and were slowly and systematically battered into submission by both heavy ground and aerial attacks. By early June it was estimated that over 200,000 Russians were killed or captured outside Kharkov. German casualties were specifically lower at 20,000 dead, wounded or missing. The Russian leadership had undoubtedly underestimated their opponent's strength here. As a direct result of their over-confidence the battle had turned into one of the most catastrophic offensives in Russian military history. The Russian defeat at Kharkov had burst open the front for the Panzerwaffe to achieve an unopposed drive south-west. Victory seemed like it was beckoning for the German commanders in the field.

(*Opposite*) Three photographs showing Pz.Kpfw IIIs on the road south-west following the defeat of Russian forces around Kharkov. This defeat of the Red Army had once more brought invincibility into the eyes of the German commanders. They now believed that the Caucasus was within their grasp, but little did they know what was in store for their forces three months later when they arrived at the banks of the River Volga overlooking the city of Stalingrad.

95

Photographed during an advance against a burning enemy target in a field is a Pz.Kpfw III belonging to the II *Abteilung* of Panzer-Regent 6 of the 3rd Panzer Division. Note the divisional insignia of the 'Berlin Bear' and the inverted 'Y' with two vertical strokes. This vehicle is an Ausf. J or L variant.

A staged image showing Panzergrenadiers in undergrowth being supported by a Pz.Kpfw III somewhere on the front lines in 1942. Although the Pz.Kpfw III made staggering successes in 1942, the eventual distances which had to be covered limited tactics as well as causing breakdowns and immense supply problems.

In southern Russia a Pz.Kpfw III passes the burning wreckage of a destroyed Russian vehicle. Operations for the Panzerwaffe in southern Russia were often quite rapid and it was regarded by the men as very good tank country. However, Panzers regularly outstripped their supplies and had to halt their furious advance, thereby wasting valuable time.

Photographed in southern Russia are Pz.Kpfw III Ausf. Ls identified by the edge of the spaced armour plate on the gun mantle. A number of Horch cross-country vehicles can be seen supporting the drive, most likely a party of staff officers.

A Pz.Kpfw III being carefully driven onto a pontoon bridge guided by one of the crew members. Logs have been tied onto the engine deck in order to help the vehicle cross marshy terrain which was often found in northern and central parts of the Soviet Union.

A decorated crewman poses for the camera next to his StuG III Ausf. B. Even by the spring of 1942 German policy still ordered that at all times assault guns were to advance with or just behind the infantry. They were never to go ahead of the infantry and when an objective was successfully reached the assault gun was to remain with the infantry while the position was being consolidated.

An excellent photograph showing the might of a Panzer division moving across the open steppe supported by aircraft. Spread out as far as the eye can see are a variety of vehicles including the Pz.Kpfw III, Horch cross-country vehicles, motorcycles and their combinations, and Opel Blitz trucks.

A Pz.Kpfw III Ausf. J has parked in front of a deserted Soviet thatched building and appears to have been temporarily occupied by German forces. Note the shirtless Panzer crewman at the rear of the tank who appears to be 'doing a call of duty'.

Out in the field is an assortment of armoured vehicles including an Sd.Kz.7/1 mounting a 2cm Flakvierling 38. This vehicle leads a column of Horch Kfz.15 and Kfz.17 cross-country cars and some Opel Blitz trucks. The Panzer that can be seen halted in the field is a Pz.Kpfw III Ausf. J.

A maintenance workshop team is salvaging parts from a knocked-out Pz.Kpfw III. The Panzer appears to be the victim of mines of large-calibre artillery as the photograph suggests a large explosion has ripped the track clean off. Note the divisional insignia painted in yellow, indicating that the vehicle belongs to the 7th Panzer Division.

An interesting photograph showing the crew of a Pz.Kpfw III and mobile maintenance engineers utilizing a log to lift up one side of the tank so that work on its undercarriage and wheels can be undertaken quickly and effectively. Special mobile maintenance units were an asset on the front lines and often salvaged vehicles or fixed them where they developed mechanical problems in order to reduce the length of time a Panzer would be out of action.

A column of Pz.Kpfw IIIs crosses a pontoon bridge somewhere in southern Russia in the late summer of 1942. Note the divisional insignia of the 24th Panzer Division on the rear of the tank. It served under the 4th Panzer Army in Army Group South on the Eastern Front. In late December 1942 it was encircled during the Battle of Stalingrad and destroyed. It was re-formed in March 1943 and served in Normandy and Italy, and then went back to the Eastern Front where it suffered heavy casualties around Kiev and the Dnepr Bend.

A column of Pz.Kpfw IIIs can be seen halted in a field. The commander of the leading tank is observed standing up in his cupola surveying the terrain ahead and trying to deduce through his 6x30 Zeiss binoculars where the enemy is sited.

Wehrmacht troops use a knocked-out Pz.Kpfw III as cover during a fire action with Soviet forces. Note the foliage still strewn across the engine deck of the tank. The use of foliage in the second year on the Eastern Front became more prominent than ever with armoured crews. Most vehicles and a large range of weapons had foliage attached to break up their distinctive shapes. The Germans soon became masters of the art of camouflaging their vehicles with branches from trees, grass and hay. In fact some vehicles carried so much foliage that it was sometimes difficult to determine what type of vehicle they were or what camouflage scheme they had.

Pictured is a typical side view of a Pz.Kpfw III deployed for action between 1941 and 1942. During this period of the war the Panzers were painted in their overall dark grey camouflage scheme (RAL 7021) which blended well with the local terrain. Painted on the side is the standard national insignia.

A knocked-out Pz.Kpfw III stands near destroyed buildings during summer operations on the Eastern Front. All the hatches of the vehicle are open, suggesting that the crew have escaped. Note the damaged track.

During operations across the vast hinterland of the Soviet Union is a column of Pz.Kpfw IIIs. Leading the drive is a pair of Ausf. Js or Ls. This photograph was probably taken in southern Russia during the summer offensive of 1942.

A Pz.Kpfw III stationary in a field encampment on the Eastern Front. Note the divisional insignia painted on the rear of the tank, indicating that it is part of the 18th Panzer Brigade of the 18th Panzer Division. The tactical number is '621'.

Pictured here in the early autumn of 1942 is a Pz.Kpfw III Ausf. G or H variant. It typically mounts a 5cm KwK gun barrel and has a commander's cupola first seen on Ausf. G models of this type.

Out in the Russian steppe in September 1942 is a Pz.Kpfw III. Note the short 5cm KwK gun barrel and the 20-litre jerry cans stored on the roof of the turret. Although difficult to ascertain due to the distance of the image, this vehicle may be an Ausf. H variant.

Out in the snow is a Pz.Kpfw III Ausf. J. The crew has applied a crude coat of winter whitewash paint on the chassis. Even during this period of the war some armoured units were still slow in adapting camouflage for their tanks.

On board a flatbed rail car destined for the front lines is a Pz.Kpfw III Ausf. H. This vehicle has received a full application of winter whitewash paint. Note the additional armoured plating clearly bolted to the lower hull. The tank is armed with a 5cm gun.

A Panzer crewman stands next to his Pz.Kpfw III. The vehicle has received a coating of winter whitewash paint which was specially designed to be thinned with water and applied to all vehicles and equipment where snow was on the ground. The application of this paint could easily be washed off by the crews in the spring, exposing the dark grey base colour. Unfortunately even during the latter period of 1942 distribution to the front lines was often delayed in some areas by a matter of weeks. Consequently, the crews had to adapt and find various crude substitutes with which to camouflage their vehicles. This included hastily applying a rough coat of lime whitewash, while others used lumps of chalk, white cloth strips and sheets, and even hand-packed snow in a drastic attempt to conceal conspicuous dark grey parts. Other vehicles, however, roamed the white arctic wilderness with no camouflage at all.

A column of Pz.Kpfw IIIs passing through a Soviet town during the winter of 1942. The vehicles all retain their factory dark grey base colour, which probably indicates they may have been freshly deployed for action.

During winter operations in 1942 and the crew of a Pz.Kpfw III Ausf. M poses for the camera. For the winter of 1942 the German army was readily supplied with winter clothing against the extreme arctic temperatures. Reversible winter uniform sheepskin garments were manufactured and supplied to the front lines. When the troops and Panzerwaffe were issued with these garments in October and November 1942, they found the clothing extremely warm and comfortable. It also provided the wearer with greater freedom of movement, especially with personal equipment. This uniform not only helped combat the severity of the cold, but helped prevent overheating during physical exertion.

A Pz.Kpfw III advances along a congested stretch of road during the depths of the winter in 1942.

Chapter Four

Relegation
1943–44

In June 1943, twenty-one Panzer divisions, including four Waffen-SS divisions and two Panzergrenadier divisions were being prepared for Operation *Zitadelle* in the Kursk salient. For this massive attack the Panzer III Ausf. L variant was fitted with spaced armoured skirts or *Schürtzen*, which was armoured plating installed around the turret and on the hull sides. However, in spite of this additional armoured protection, the Panzer IV, Tiger and the new Panther were to play the most dominant role in the battle of Kursk. In total there were seventeen divisions and two brigades with no less than 1,715 Panzers and 147 StuG III assault guns. Each division averaged some ninety-eight Panzers and self-propelled anti-tank guns. The new Pz.Kpfw V Panther Ausf. A made its debut, despite its production problems.

Initially the German armoured attack at Kursk went well, with the Panzer III scoring sizeable successes along some parts of the front. However, within only a matter of days, strong Soviet defensive positions consisting of literally hundreds of anti-tank guns had ground down the mighty Panzerwaffe and threw its offensive timetable off-schedule. Through sheer weight of Soviet strength and stubborn combat along an ever-extending front, the German mobile units were finally forced to a standstill.

As a direct result, the reverberations caused by the defeat at Kursk meant that German forces in the south bore the brunt of the heaviest Soviet drive. Both the Russian Voronezh and Steppe Fronts possessed massive local superiority against everything the Germans had on the battlefield, and this included their diminishing resources of tanks and assault guns. The Panzerwaffe were now duty-bound to improvise with what they had at their disposal and try to maintain themselves in the field, and in so doing they hoped to wear the enemy's offensive capacity.

By the winter of 1943 diminishing armoured units continued to fight on an ever-extended front. Due to the introduction of the up-gunned and up-armoured Panzer IV, the Panzer III was slowly relegated to secondary roles such as training, and it was replaced as the main German medium tank by the Panzer IV and Panther.

Even so, the Pz.Kpfw III continued to see extended combat on all fronts, despite its relegation. German tank units, despite the dire situation, were still infused with confidence and the ability to hold ground. Grim as the situation was, armoured units were compelled to try to fill the gaps left by the infantry, and hold the front to the death. Throughout November and December 1943 the Panzerwaffe fought well and at times even succeeded in surprising Red Army forces with a number of daring attacks of their own. Although handicapped from the onset by their lack of reserves, the Panzers continued to try to hold ground and even managed at times to spearhead a number of attacks, causing considerable losses to Soviet armour.

Although German Panzerwaffe commanders were fully aware of the fruitless attempts by its forces to establish a defensive line, the crews followed instructions implicitly in a number of areas to halt the Soviet drive. Again and again Panzer units fought to the death. A mass of infantry, mixed with the remnants of naval and Luftwaffe groups, supported the motorized columns as they fought against innumerable numbers of Russian tanks. Many of the German armoured vehicles were festooned with camouflage, and wherever possible moved under the cover of trees or the cover of night to avoid being attacked by the Red Army Air Force, which had almost total control of the air over the Eastern Front.

By the summer of 1944, desperation began to grip the front lines even further. Little in the way of reinforcements reached the Germans, and those that were left holding a defensive position had already been forced into various ad hoc Panzer divisions that were simply thrown together with a handful of tanks and Panzer-grenadiers. Many of these hastily-formed formations were short-lived. The majority were either completely decimated in the fighting or had received such a mauling in battle that they were reorganized into a different ad hoc formation under a new commander. Fervent efforts to increase the combat strength of the Panzerwaffe, Panzer units and individuals of Panzer and Panzergrenadier divisions were under-taken, but these were too exhausted to avert the situation decisively. As a result the Russians continued pushing forward, while German forces retreated westward. Destruction seemed destined to unfold.

Two crew members of a Pz.Kpfw III crew stand in front of their whitewashed Panzer during the early winter of 1943. Throughout the early cold months of 1943 the Panzerwaffe built up the strength of the badly depleted Panzer divisions.

Out in the field supporting troops dressed in winter white camouflage suits is a whitewashed Pz.Kpfw III. The troops' two-piece snowsuits were shapeless outfits comprising a snow jacket and matching trousers.

Out on the Northern Front near Leningrad a knocked-out Russian tank can be seen. A column of support vehicles can be indentified moving along a road to support positions around the besieged city. During this period of the war the Germans were well aware that if the hold on Leningrad were broken, Army Group North would eventually lose control of the Baltic Sea. Finland would be isolated, supplies of iron ore from Sweden would be in danger, and the U-boat training programme would be seriously curtailed. It was now imperative that the troops held the front and wage a static battle of attrition until other parts of the Russian front could be stabilized.

The Waffen-SS crew of a Pz.Kpfw III is pictured during the battle of Kharkov in March 1943. These SS Panzer and Panzergrenadier divisions had become known as the 'fire brigade' of the Third Reich. Wherever they were committed to battle, they attacked. Sometimes the outcome was successful and there were many times when they failed, but whatever the outcome of the individual action, the end mostly resulted in delaying the enemy advance. In March 1943 three elite Waffen-SS divisions, *Leibstandarte Adolf Hitler*, *Das Reich* and *Totenkopf* of the newly-formed SS Panzer Corps recaptured the city of Kharkov.

A Pz.Kpfw III wades across a small river during early spring operations on the Eastern Front. By the spring of 1943 the German forces were holding a battle line more than 1,400 miles in overall length which had been severely weakened by the overwhelming strength of the Red Army. To make matters worse, during the first half of 1943 Panzerwaffe units were finding it harder and harder to be refitted with proper replacements to compensate for the large losses sustained. Supplies of equipment and ammunition were also becoming insufficient in some areas of the front. However, by mid-1943 the Panzerwaffe was slowly restored with an arsenal of armour of some twenty-four Panzer divisions on the Eastern Front alone. This was a staggering transformation of a Panzer force that had lost immeasurable amounts of armour in less than two years of combat.

A variety of armoured vehicles in the field comprising Pz.Kpfw IIs, IIIs, IVs and halftracks. These vehicles are purposely spread out to make an aerial attack against their advancing unit more difficult.

Three SS crewmen pose for the camera on board their new Pz.Kpfw III Ausf. L somewhere on the Eastern Front.

An SS officer holding the rank of an SS-*Untersturmführer* poses for the camera in front of what is probably a new Pz.Kpfw III Ausf. L.

SS crewmen have their photograph taken with another Pz.Kpfw III Ausf. L of the same SS unit. Note the name 'Ernest Stammler' painted on the side of the tank, probably in honour of a fallen comrade.

A Pz.Kpfw III crew ensure that their Panzer is not detected by aerial or ground enemy reconnaissance and foliage is applied to help conceal it.

A Panzergrenadier takes cover near an Sd.Kfz.251 halftrack during the opening phase of Operation *Zitadelle*. This was to be the largest tank battle ever fought in the history of warfare. The plan was for the German forces to smash Red Army formations and leave the road to Moscow open. For this daring offensive the German force was distributed between the Northern and Southern groups, consisting of a total of twenty-two divisions, six of which were Panzer and five Panzergrenadier.

A Pz.Kpfw III with troops riding on board who are being transported to the front lines. At Kursk both the Wehrmacht and Panzerwaffe caused considerable destruction against the first lines of Russian defence. As a direct result of the German ferocity, condition of the Red Army troops varied considerably. While some areas of the front were demoralized and often without sufficient weapons, others parts were heavily defended with a formidable force.

A battery of StuG IIIs have been secured ready for transport on a flatbed rail car during the summer of 1943. By this period of the war instead of the StuG being a weapon for primarily supporting the infantry, it had become yet another defensive weapon with its main task to kill tanks.

A StuG III advancing along a dusty road towards the front lines in the summer of 1943. By early 1943 the StuG had become a very popular assault gun, especially on the Eastern Front. Its low profile and mechanical reliability saw its employment grow on the battlefield. Some 3,041 of them were operational in 1943 alone.

Pictured here across the vast steppe are Pz.Kpfw IIIs and IVs advancing into action during the battle of Kursk. Note the interesting summer camouflage schemes and side-skirt armour. These vehicles have been given the new three-colour paint scheme and the crews have applied them in stripes. By 1943 olive green was being used on vehicles, weapons and large pieces of equipment. A red-brown colour RAL 8012 had also been introduced at the same time. These two colours, along with a new colour base of dark yellow RAL 7028, were issued to crews in the form of a highly-concentrated paste. This arrived in 2kg and 20kg cans and units were ordered to apply the paste over the entire surface of the vehicle. The substance was specially adapted so that it could be thinned with water or even fuel and could be applied by spray, brush or mop.

An interesting photograph during the battle of Kursk in the northern sector showing a large column of armoured vehicles advancing across a field. Visible are the Sd.Kfz.251 halftracks, Pz.Kpfw II, III and Sd.Kfz.10 halftrack mounting a flak gun. The initial phase of the northern thrust went well, with the Germans slowly and systematically bulldozing their way through while Russian troops either fought to the death or saved themselves by escaping the impending slaughter by withdrawing to another makeshift position. Fighting on the northern front was a fierce contest of attrition, and although the Red Army had showed great fortitude and determination, they were constantly hampered by overwhelming firepower from Tiger and Panther tanks.

During a temporary lull in the fighting the crew of a Pz.Kpfw III makes minor repairs to their vehicle. During the battle of Kursk seven Panzer divisions in total were annihilated with terrible effect on the German war effort. The offensive was a catastrophe for the German forces on the Eastern Front. Hitler had chosen an objective that was far too ambitious. The attack had also been continually delayed, allowing Russian forces additional time to prepare their defensive positions in the salient. Despite German efforts to batter their way through, they had neither the strength nor resources to do so. The cream of the German Panzer force, so carefully concentrated prior to the operation, was exhausted and the Russians had undeniably gained the initiative in the East forever.

Armoured vehicles comprising mainly Pz.Kpfw IVs going forward into action during the latter phase of Kursk. Both the Pz.Kpfw III and larger Pz.Kpfw IV fought well during the summer offensive, but the Soviet defences comprising many thousands of tank mines and anti-tank guns had caused considerable casualties, almost ending any future for the Pz.Kpfw III as a main battle tank. It was now down to the powerful Tiger and new Panther tanks to try to restore the war effort in the east.

A Pz.Kpfw III command tank has halted on the steppe with other armoured vehicles during the latter period of the Kursk offensive. The reverberations caused by the German defeat at Kursk meant that German forces in the south bore the brunt of the heaviest Soviet drive. Both the Russian Voronezh and Steppe Fronts possessed massive local superiority against everything the Germans had on the battlefield and this included their diminishing resources of tanks and assault guns.

An interesting photograph showing Waffen-SS troops dug-in along a position in the summer of 1943. A Pz.Kpfw III passes the position on its way to the front. In these last years the deciding factors in ground warfare were the Panzer, self-propelled artillery and mechanized infantry. The Waffen-SS played a key part in trying to hold significant ground. These elite combat formations saw extensive action and were continuously being shuttled from one danger spot to another with only brief respite for refitting.

In Army Group South an interesting photograph showing a Panzer crew applying whitewash paint to their late variant Pz.Kpfw III. Note the smoke-candle dischargers attached to the tank's turret. Throughout January and February 1944 the winter did nothing to impede the Soviet offensives from grinding further west. At the beginning of March 1944 Army Group South supported by armour still held about half the ground between the Dnepr and Bug, but in a number of areas the front was buckling under the constant strain of repeated Soviet attacks. As a consequence Army Group South was being slowly pressed westwards, its Panzers still unable to strike a decisive counter-blow because of the Führer's order to stand fast on unsuitable positions.

Whitewashed Pz.Kpfw IIIs advance along the front lines during winter operations in early 1944. During this period the Germans held significant ground and by the early spring mud finally brought an end to almost continuous fighting and there was respite for the Panzerwaffe in some areas of the front. In addition to this, the armaments industry had begun producing many new vehicles for the Eastern Front. In fact during 1944 the Panzerwaffe were better supplied with equipment than during any other time on the Eastern Front, thanks to the efforts of the armaments industry. In total some 20,000 fighting vehicles including 8,328 medium and heavy tanks, 5,751 assault guns, 3,617 tank destroyers and 1, 246 self-propelled artillery carriages of various types reached the Eastern Front.

An interesting photograph showing an SS crewman posing for the camera next to his brand-new whitewashed Pz.Kpfw III Ausf. M during the winter of 1943. Note the divisional emblem of the 1st SS Panzergrenadier Division 'LSSAH' painted on the front plate of the vehicle.

Another Pz.Kpfw III Ausf. M belonging to the 1st SS Panzergrenadier Division 'LSSAH' during operations in Russia in the winter of 1943.

The crew of a Pz.Bef.Wg III Ausf. H standing next to their machine during winter operations on the Eastern Front in 1943. Note the 'Berlin Bear' emblem indicating that this vehicle belongs to Panzer Regiment 35 of the 4th Panzer Division.

Chapter Five

End Game
1944–45

By the summer of 1944 the German army on the Eastern Front was fighting for survival. It was in the summer that the Soviets unleashed Operation Bagration – the Russian code-name for the 1944 summer offensive, which was to eventually lead to the wholesale destruction of the German Army Group Centre. This massive Russian offensive opened up three years to the day after Germany's 1941 invasion of the Soviet Union. Fighting over many of the same battlefields, German troops found themselves battling to the death in a desperate attempt to prevent the mighty Red Army forces from re-capturing Byelorussia, the last bastion of defence for the Germans before Poland. The Bagration offensive which Army Group Centre was compelled to attempt to counter was a swift and bloodthirsty battle of attrition which resulted in a catastrophe of unbelievable proportions. For days and weeks German soldiers, still determined to fight to the bitter end, had to endure the constant hammer blows of ground and aerial bombardments plus endless armoured and infantry attacks. Although many German units continued to fight a grim defence, the Red Army had already punched a line allowing an almost seemingly unstoppable flood, pushing apart and encircling many vital German Panzer and infantry divisions. In the end Bagration cost the Wehrmacht more men and material than the catastrophe at Stalingrad sixteen months earlier. This shattering defeat of Army Group Centre saw the loss of over 300,000 men and resulted in Soviet forces pushing back exhausted German remnants out of Russia through Poland to the gates of Warsaw.

The destruction of Army Group Centre in the summer of 1944 has been completely overshadowed by the Normandy campaign, which was unleashed just three weeks prior to Bagration along the shores of northern France. The battle which the German forces endured on the Eastern Front that fateful summer was more catastrophic than that on the Western Front.

By the late summer of 1944 the military situation on the Eastern Front was calamitous and it was fast becoming clear, even to the least knowledgeable German soldier, how rapidly their army was diminishing. The absence of communications too made it impossible for the Germans to realize the full extent of the ongoing disintegration. There seemed no stopping the tide of the Russian advance, and as they remorselessly pushed forward German formations became increasingly confused and entangled in bitter bloody fighting. In some areas the fighting was so fierce that it was virtually impossible to distinguish between friend and foe. Engagements like this had been fought scores of times on the Eastern Front, but many believed never with such ferocity.

In spite of the terrible setbacks on the Eastern Front, the Pz.Kpfw III continued to prove its worthiness on the battlefield. However, it was too lightly armoured to do anything more than support defending front lines against the advancing storm of the Red Army.

In order to strengthen the diminishing Panzerwaffe the Germans went to great lengths to modify various Panzer chassis. Apart from the successful introduction of the StuG III, the Germans increased the use of self-propelled mounts on either the chassis of the Pz.Kpfw III or the IV. Back in 1942 there had been a drastic requirement for the need of motorized artillery to be deployed in action at a moment's notice. For this reason the Germans adopted the concept of self-propelled artillery mounts such as the heavy field 15cm howitzer mounted on a tank. There was also the *Flammpanzer* III Ausf. M/Panzer III (F1), which was a flamethrower tank. Around 100 of these were converted from existing Panzer III Ausf. M, but did little in suppressing Red Army attacks. In addition to this there was the *Bergepanzer* III. In 1944 some Panzer IIIs were converted to armoured recovery vehicles. However, the majority were mainly issued to formations with Tiger I tanks. There was also the *Artillerie-Panzerbeobachtungswagen* III, which was a forward artillery observer tank, and 262 of these were produced.

Although many of these variants saw extensive action, their success as a whole was very limited and localized and did nothing to avert enemy operations. Over the next weeks and months a dramatic decline in the Panzerwaffe continued as supplies and fuel became even scarcer. German units and stragglers tried in vain with varying degrees of courage and determination to suppress their foe. As they endeavoured to break out west the majority of troops were forced to abandon most of their heavy equipment and weapons. As a result there were frequent scenes of chaos and disorganization as they advanced westward along roads, paths and fields trying to escape from the jaws of the Red Army.

As for the Panzer III, by 1945 very few were seen in service as many of them had either been knocked out of action, were relegated into training, or had been simply transformed into up-gunned self-propelled artillery mounts in desperation to stave off the end of the war.

A whitewashed Pz.Kpfw III command vehicle with intact side-skirts advances across a frozen plain somewhere on the Eastern Front. While most Pz.Kpfw IIIs had been relegated to training duties or were modified into self-propelled vehicles, there were still some of the tanks found on the front. All of these vehicles would have to be irrevocably stretched along a very thin Eastern Front with many of them rarely reaching the proper operating level. Panzer divisions too were often broken up and split among hastily-constructed battle groups or *Kampfgruppe* drawn from a motley collection of armoured formations, but still these battle groups were put into the line operating well below strength.

Panzergrenadiers wearing their distinctive white snow suits use a knocked-out T/34 as cover in the open steppe of the Eastern Front. Bleak as the situation was, armoured units supported the Panzergrenadiers' drive and quite often were compelled to try to fill the gaps left by the troops and hold the front to the grim death. Regularly-armoured crews fought well and at times even succeeded in surprising Red Army forces with a number of daring attacks of their own.